The Whistle Always Blew At Noon

The Whistle Always Blew At Noon

C Gamble

Copyrights © 2023

All Rights Reserved

No part of this book may be reproduced or transmitted in any form or by any means, electronic or mechanical, including photocopying, recording, or by any information storage and retrieval system without the written permission of the author, except where permitted by law.

This manuscript is dedicated to the memories of Mike, Bill, and Dennis.

Preface

The author arrived in Williams Bay, Wisconsin as a midterm 5th grader in the year 1960. It was his seventh school since enrolling in kindergarten in his place of birth – Beloit, Wisconsin. Having arrived in the Bay with no expectations of a lengthy residence, he was actually afforded nearly five years of stability and prosperity. When asked, "Where did you grow up?" he would say, "I grew up in the Bay". Although the family picked up stakes and relocated to Green Bay after the author just completed his freshman year, Williams Bay has always been his "home is where the heart is" home. As such, the beautiful two-story house on Elm Street became the "old house," and the Bay will always be "home."

Over the years, he has been reminded by friends how much he has fondly described living in the picturesque village known as Williams Bay. As is often the case, a person takes the suggestion "you should write about it" with a grain of salt. That, for a number of years, was just the case with this author. Having a reasonably good education but possessing limited writing skills and writing experiences, there were impediments that had to be challenged and overcome. So, what changed his mind (what pushed him over the edge)? Having a health crisis and nothing but time on his hands, he decided to take the plunge.

This story is one that could actually be told by anyone who has been raised in a small town in America. But, the author unabashedly asserts Williams Bay was unlike any other. The physical, social, and cultural characteristics of the Bay represent anything and everything Rockwellian.

For a growing boy, the town provided all the support, nurturance, and guidance to prepare him for the obstacle course called adult life. The words of William Wordsworth seem apropos – "The child is the father of the man."

The author makes no claim as to the literary quality, or lack thereof, as it pertains to this essay. A Pulitzer, it is not. What it is, though, is a heartfelt story, a nostalgic road trip, if you will. For the author, the tale the reader is asked to digest is a trip down memory lane that was too visceral, too personally compelling not to write.

The small sample of anecdotes provides a glimpse into the life of a young boy growing up in a very special place. No excuses are issued for the raw simplicity of the events described. Yes – the boy did break his bedroom window, courtesy of an errantly thrown baseball. He and his chums fished off the town pier, took bike rides to the nearby village of Fontana, sneaked onto the golf course, frequented the clear waters of the village beach, and took the 26-mile walk around Lake Geneva…

It was just time for the septuagenarian to write, reminisce, and celebrate his time spent with his dear friends.

Do you remember the time… do you remember when…

The Whistle Always Blew At Noon

Back in the day, there were no traffic signals, just stop signs. Stop signs alerted traffic on Highway 67 that Highway 50 motorists had the right-of-way. Geographically, that intersection, actually a glacial ground moraine, serves as the portal to Williams Bay or just "The Bay." Officially, the Bay begins near the Fieldhouse, where a sign alerts incoming traffic to the latest population of the village. Many times, and over the many years, the former resident, now an aging adult (a.k.a. old man), has made the journey "back home." Periodically, he has pondered the simple question – Why go back? What do you expect to see? And so forth. The answers always seemed elusive as the questions were obviously rhetorical. As if a dimmable bulb turns bright, reality hits the old man. It is not the old man who makes the pilgrimage. He is simply transporting a young boy back home, back home to a childhood that has been cherished – never dulled by the passing of time. So, the questions have been answered, and the purpose of the visits is defined.

As the old man begins his descent down Highway 67 toward the village, the boy recognizes the typical southern

Wisconsin landmarks. Farms with their whitewashed barns occupy much of the landscape, with the chief residents being those black and white dairy cows known as Holsteins. What used to seem like a generous distance to town, is traveled in minutes. Nonetheless, the boy sees the old landmarks. Can't miss the Fieldhouse, Steins (with the blue canvas awning in front), and the Arctic Circle. Shortly, the firehouse comes into view. Adjacent is Luke's Restaurant, the warmest place in town when delivering newspapers on a cold winter morning.

He remembers a particularly cold morning when he was delivering the Chicago Tribune newspaper. Just another cold Wisconsin morning. The paper had to be "stuffed" with those annoying and cumbersome ads. After all, what difference did it make what was on sale in Chicago? With his baskets chocked full of newspapers, he coaxed his bike to cooperate on that cold, dark morning. Usually, the restaurant, Luke's Restaurant, was his first or second stop. He recalls opening the restaurant door only to be greeted by this friendly, concerned, diminutive woman he assumed to be the owner. Before he could exit, she insisted the boy sit down, take off his coat, and enjoy the warmth emanating from the kitchen area. Reluctantly, he complied with what was obviously no longer a suggestion but a firmly stated command – "Young man, you sit down and have some toast and hot chocolate!" The boy was not sorry for his decision to comply even though he worried about falling behind schedule. After all, he was packing extra weight with those annoying weekend sales ads. The warmth and sustenance he availed himself of was not measured in terms of the temperature in the restaurant. Rather, it was the extension of consideration and kindness the boy would learn over the years that was emblematic of his home – the Bay.

As in previous years, the boy's trips have had a routine, as he has a number of stops to make. Always first, and without exception, a visit to the old house takes precedence. The old man pulls into the library parking lot. The boy can see across the street the house on Elm Street, the "old house," which was once occupied by the Gamble family. Still, a beautiful home neatly tucked between Miss Kellman's and Mrs. Peterson's.

The boy gazes upon that second-story window and flashes back to a lazy summer afternoon. It was that afternoon he was feeling a little bored and wanted to play a game of catch. With no friends around that day, he took matters into his own hands. All he needed was a ball and a glove. Standing and facing the house, he proceeded to throw the ball on the roof above the porch. It wasn't a real game of catch, but it sufficed until an errant throw shattered his bedroom window. Understandably, panic set in. After inspecting the damage and pausing for some serious head-scratching, he did the only logical thing he could. The wastebasket provided a method of disposing of the damning evidence. After measuring the opening, he hot-footed it down to the hardware store to purchase the requisite window pane. He was quite relieved upon the successful completion of his project. Just one thing – he neglected to discretely dispose of the evidence. When the boy's father got home, the boy got an earful.

The boy cannot count the number of times he wanted to knock on the door of his boyhood home. He wasn't sure what he would say except to explain the history of "his" home as it related to his growing up under that very roof. Leery of what might be the homeowner's reaction, the boy has never executed the gesture. Really, the boy is mostly interested in taking a peek in the backyard. The very back of the property was defined by a white picket fence that bordered Ms. Steele's home on Spring Street. Hours and hours were spent in that backyard, most of which involved wiffle ball games with his chums. He can clearly remember his Black Labrador "Spike" playing shortstop – probably the best shortstop in town.

The first leg of the journey is in the books. In no hurry, the boy gazes upon the library, remembering it as an aging gray building. Where the boy is standing now is remembered as a vacant lot and the site of a number of pickup baseball games. The library's interior was somewhat dusty and dimly lit, possessing a kind of solemnity. The boy did not spend as much time in the library as he should have. There were more active pursuits competing for his attention, most of which satisfied his yearning to be in the outdoors. His sister did, however, spend a number of hours helping Mrs. Pierce organize and stack books. In doing so, Mrs. Pierce taught her the fundamentals of the Dewey decimal system. Oddly, he does remember the first book he checked out and read from cover-to-cover *Slide Danny Slide!* (a book about baseball, of course).

The boy takes additional time to peer down Geneva Street, remembering the various businesses. Across from the library, looking toward Geneva St., was the Standard Station, Cities Service Station, and, of course, Doc Wiswell's office. Just across the street from Doc's office was a small white two-bedroom house. The modest structure represented the boy's family's initial residence in the Bay. It wasn't much, but it was an auspicious start. Behind the house, on the same property, were three or four summer cottages the boy's mother managed in the Summer months. Upon the family's arrival that chilly spring day, was a laborious task, one the boy was all too familiar with-- the unloading and organizing of the family possessions. Nearing the end of the day, the boy's father informed him there was a lake just down the street. The boy's eyes lit up, and he asked for permission to explore some. Down Geneva Street he went, passing the Pure Service station on the right and "downtown" on the left. Proceeding further, he passed Luke's Restaurant; parked in front was that wooden bench with the phrase carved into the seat that stated: "set for a spell." From Luke's, past the fire station, he went, finally arriving at the lake. She (the Bay) was huge, he thought, not yet knowing what he was seeing was just a portion of the lake. The breeze of the spring day moved the water vigorously, and the scent emanating from the wave action would be forever embedded in his senses. As he stared out at the newfound body of water, he was mesmerized. The boy was anxious to head back up the hill so as to describe his discovery. Little did he know, this was just the beginning of many explorations and discoveries to come. As he would learn, the Bay possessed a plethora of interesting places. The boy remembers virtually all of them as if it were yesterday and captured on Kodachrome.

Time to move on. The old man, with the boy in tow, ventured further up Geneva Street. The sojourn would not be complete without a stop at the old school or Yerkes Observatory. The observatory first. The manicured grounds and the imposing buildings were pristine, just as he remembers. The old man is well aware of the significance and history of the observatory. The critical fact relates to the telescope housed in the largest of the domes. Then and still today, the observatory is well known in the scientific community for possessing the largest refracting telescope in the world. It was the boy's sixth-grade class that was allowed passage into the inner sanctum. On that clear, moonless night, each student was given the opportunity of a lifetime to look through the massive instrument and gaze into the deep recesses of the universe.

While the observatory held educational and scientific significance, those beautiful grounds deserve special notice. On a more mundane note, the boy can look out on those grounds and see his chums choosing sides for another baseball or football game. It was the usual collection of youngsters as the scene rivaled that of the movie *Sandlot*, with the boys dressed in those horizontally striped shirts accompanied by high-top black sneakers and blue jeans.

No trip would be complete without a visit to the old school. The two companions proceed back down Geneva St. As the boy peers out the window, he sees what was then one of the newer homes back in the 1960s. He recalls his friend Tom (Buzz) and his family being the occupants. Unexpectedly, his chauffeur turns left onto Hill St. He quickly realizes the car is slowing down in front of a house the boy spent untold hours in. His friend Dennis and his family occupied the home during the boy's years in the Bay. Dennis' mom worked at the dry goods store in town, while Dennis' dad was a carpenter. The boy had the utmost affection for both. They treated the boy as if he was one of their own. Dennis was as good a chum as anyone could ask for. The boy and Dennis were polar opposites. Dennis was outgoing, mischievous to a fault – probably hyperactive by today's standards.

It was a picturesque summer day when he received a phone call from Dennis persuading him to meet up for a round of golf. Just two problems. Den had a cast on his left arm, and neither "golfer" had sufficient funds to support their endeavor. Not to be deterred, Den cut his cast so he could slide the encumbrance up to his bicep and swing accordingly. No funds – no problem. Dennis discovered a passage to the golf course through an opening in the woods on the observatory grounds.

Everything was copesetic until the two observed a small moving object increasing in size until they were engaged by the golf course pro. The gentleman issued the two delinquents a tongue-lashing but spared them from any serious consequences. The boy remembers this incident as just one of the many adventures he experienced with his pal Dennis.

The old man returns to Geneva St., turning onto Congress St. and stopping in front of the old, weathered brick building. The old man parked across the street from the gym and cafeteria entrance. His rental vehicle is occupying spaces unofficially reserved for the upperclassmen vehicles back in the day. The boy was impressed with a number of those cars. Not knowing their specific vintages, some looked like those having been driven by Eliot Ness. That crop of upperclassmen had a real penchant for cars. The most memorable of the lot was a jalopy that was bright red, had no hood, and was dubbed the "tired tomato."

When the boy focuses on those old traffic-worn entrances, the nostalgic images pop up like a slideshow from a carousel projector. Five special years of mental pictures compete for his attention. The boy could write a book (probably no one would read it but himself anyway) about his experiences in that building. For now, he is simply enjoying the uninterrupted time to reminisce. It is ironic that the recollections of such pleasant times almost always move the old man nearly to tears. A peculiar feeling comes over the old man. It is time to move along to other venues, but the memories keep begging him to stay. The boy, now sixty-some years later, must say goodbye and leave those life experiences to fend for themselves, but not until he pauses further to allow the old man a few moments to appreciate the mentorship and guidance of the very people that make a school a school – the teachers.

The boy's recollection of his teachers, his teachers from the 5th through the 9th grade, occupy a copious amount of film. So many of his teachers have left a lasting impression. Some left more than an impression – some created indelible marks that are more like tattoos etched in the boy's educational hard drive. Mrs. Eliot was just one of those people. Mrs. E. taught a combined 5th and 6th-grade class. The boy was one of her 6th-grade students. Mrs. E. was a middle-aged woman with dark hair streaked with intermittent gray. She always arranged her hair in what was called a bun. Short in stature, Mrs. E. possessed boundless energy. In retrospect, the old man recalls maybe being a bit smitten with his tireless mentor. It was occasional, but all too often, Mrs. E.'s husband would visit her classroom. He was just a pest as far as the boy was concerned. To this day, the old man regards Mrs. E. as one of the best and always holds her in the highest esteem. It was nothing short of a privilege to be one of her students.

Mrs. Eliot skillfully prepared that 6th class for the next important step – Junior High School. Now, it was Mrs. Johnson's turn. Mrs. Johnson ran her classroom like a tight ship. A very deft, no-nonsense teacher, Mrs. J. covered the core subjects.

English was her forte. The old man remembers laboring over her homework assignments, especially those that included diagramming sentences. Math, science, and so forth were handed off to other teachers, others such as Mr. Scherff. All the way through grade school, the boy had exclusively female teachers. Mr. Scherff took some getting used to. Mr. Scherff possessed a prominent stern look. As looks can be deceiving, that was certainly the case with Mr. Scherff. Usually dressed in his PE attire, he sported a polo shirt, coaching slacks, and shoes with unique soles resembling tractor treads. Although Mr. Scherff taught math and health classes, he was generally spotted in the gym. The boy quickly became more at ease with Mr. Scherff, as his new, favorite teacher had a knack for using sarcasm, much like the boy's father. So, wisecracks and quips were observed as part and parcel of Mr. Scherff's teaching arsenal.

The cadre of memories of his teachers seems endless, too many to recount, but he would be remiss if Mr. Thompson was left out of the conversation. Mr. Thompson deserves a place at the old man's nostalgic table for several reasons. First, he was the boy's 7th-grade shop teacher. The shop was one of the boy's favorite classes - no homework, no test. Second, he was the administrator of the beach and beach house during the summer vacation. Thus, he was present year-round. As a teacher, Mr. Thompson left no doubt as to who was in charge in his dusty domain. Having a somewhat intimidating disposition, he was the pro's pro of the teaching ranks. Any shop teacher worth their salt must be a stickler for detail. Mr. T. was no exception, in spades. For example, before initiating any project, each student was required to pass the customary test – "squaring the board." The boy managed to cross that bridge and commenced working on his project. By the end of the year, the project was successfully completed and is, to this day, proudly displayed in the old man's home.

And so that term, that first year of junior high school, was in the books, but that was not the last of Mr. Thompson. Even in a small town like Williams Bay, teachers were rarely seen until the resumption of classes after Labor Day. Mr. T., on the other hand, was encountered by anyone who frequented the beach. The village beach, a public beach, on any summer day, competed with the Municipal Pier as one of the busiest places in the village. And so, the boy would frequently run in to his shop teacher, Mr. T (out of uniform, so to speak), at the entrance to the beach house. He saw a very different side to his demanding shop teacher. To his surprise, Mr. T. could actually be a very jocular gent. He, for some unknown reason, greeted the adolescent – "Hi Philadelphia, how are you today?" Was this his shop teacher or someone impersonating the gray-haired man he knew as the stoic Mr. Thompson? The boy, apparently now "Philadelphia," responded with disguised irritation, eventually became desensitized, and actually appreciated the special attention. He still did not understand the origins of such an oblique moniker.

It is now approaching the noon hour. The boy expects to hear the noon whistle; the old man is not so sure. The fire station whistle always blew at noon and served as a useful reminder, no matter where the boy was or what he was doing, the morning was concluded.

The old man locates a local eatery kitty corner from the fire station. The sign says Harpoon Willie's but the boy recognizes it as the old Hollister Lumber Yard. Seating is self-serve, so the old man finds a window seat with a view of the park. Somewhere along the line, it was officially named Edgewater Park. To the boy and his chums, it was just called the "park." The boy gazes out the window while the old man tackles his beer and sandwich. What the boy sees is the customary activity with a number of kids engaging the playground equipment. Always popular, the swing set is fully occupied. The merry-go-round and slide are also attracting the usual attention.

The park was not just for kids. During the summer months, adults were known to frequent the area. This was especially true when some of the townsfolk would gather on a warm summer night to observe the Williams Bay fire department do battle with a fire department from a nearby town. With fire hoses ready for battle, the object was to move a metal barrel, suspended by a cable, from one end to the other. Scores were kept, and town pride was at stake. Perhaps dull by today's entertainment standards, the event invariably drew quite the crowd.

The old man finishes his lunch and contemplates the next leg of the journey. The boy is eyeing the far end of the park where the simple wooden bridge has, for years, provided passage to the lakefront and other desired locales. The old man walks across the street, eventually reaching the fire station. One question of the day has been answered. Disappointingly, the whistle did not blow at noon. The old man wonders when the last time the noon whistle was heard. The boy often relied on that whistle as he never carried a wristwatch. For nostalgic reasons, the old man hoped the tradition was not retired unceremoniously.

As the two traverse the park, the boy recalls donning his PF Flyers or Red Ball Jets and heading toward the old wooden bridge. On a cool summer morning, the thick dew drops would conspire to soak his canvas tennis shoes. The bridge requires respite and contemplation. The boy, usually accompanied by a fellow towhead or two, would stop on the bridge and attempt to locate their quarry. Armed with fishing poles, tackle boxes, and minnow buckets, the boys would stop at the first of the three bait shops and liveries. Carlson's was the first. One could purchase live bait or rent a boat. One of the boys would ask the attendant for a half dozen crappie minnows. Minnows were pricey – 20 cents a dozen. The boy would hand him a dime and request a half dozen, wherein he would proceed to fill the bucket to the brim. The gentleman would always ask the boys if they needed any worms or nightcrawlers. There was no need for nightcrawlers – they were procured the night before with the aid of a flashlight and Folgers coffee can. Once completing the transaction at the bait shop, the boys would proceed expeditiously to the pier so as to claim their "spot."

Now, the old man walks at a leisurely pace. No need to hurry without the press of fishing. So, out to the end of the pier, the two go. The Municipal Pier, as it is called now, was just called the "pier" and harbors a bumper crop of fond memories. The boy can picture himself and his fellow towheads occupying the pier pretty much unmolested throughout most of the mornings they fished their favorite spot. The guys didn't usually fish much beyond mid-morning, as their solitude was often invaded by commerce.

The boy can look out the end of the pier and see the mailboat approaching. Soon, it will be followed by those darn excursion boats. He and his serious fishermen cohorts felt insulted by the presence of both. Equally culpable, the unwelcomed vessels managed to puncture the morning calm with their loud motors and resultant wake. Before the new pier was constructed, the old pier was immediately adjacent to the beach. It was a rickety old thing, and those vessels would shake the moorings vigorously. The boys were often surprised and relieved it held up under the assault of those unwanted intruders. One thing was for sure: the fishing off that antique was decidedly better.

It was one fairly uneventful day – just another peaceful, calm summer morning, really. The only difference, as the boy recalls, is that it was a Saturday. The young, dedicated fishermen usually regarded a summer weekend day as one that was rudely commandeered by the boating enthusiasts, and thus, Saturdays and Sundays were avoided. That particular day was an exception as the boy's chum, Mike, insisted on fishing – "The crappies are biting." Both nimrods were having some success. The quiet of the morning was abruptly terminated when the boy felt an incredible tug on his fishing pole. The trouble was it was on his back cast. He turned around to investigate the delay, only to discover he had hooked Mike in the back of the head. Unbelievably, Mike did not let out a whimper but simply asked to be released from the pressure of the fishing line. Delicately, trying not to hurt his chum, the boy unclipped the Silver Spoon from the swivel, leaving the hook in Mike's scalp. Next thing – "Get the **** hook out of my head." Luckily, back in the day, boys' hairstyles usually supported the pineapple look. There's nothing to really comb, just stubble. That should have made the hook extraction a piece of cake.

After several attempts, the two boys were no closer to success than when they started. Mike suggested a visit to Doc Wiswell's office should do the trick. So up the hill on Geneva Street, the boys went. Suddenly, just in front of the Post Office, Mike stopped. He declared an end to the journey and, with a commanding jerk, extracted the unwanted object from his scalp. His reasoning was sound, "What are we thinking? It's Saturday, and Doc's office is closed." With blood in copious amounts, normal for a scalp wound, exiting the injury site, the two boys reversed course and headed back to the pier (Mike was worried about someone helping themselves to their prized fishing equipment). Eventually, the fishing was concluded, but Mike never ever mentioned the incident, nor did he express any upset. It wouldn't be the last time the two boys would wet a line together, but the following trips were less eventful in that regard.

Whenever the boy and his chums would fish the pier, they customarily picked up stakes around 10 AM. By then, the cotton rope stringer had a sizable catch for the day – usually bluegills, crappie, and perch. To conclude their fishing trip, invariably, one of the boys would declare, "Time to go." Without hesitation, one of the boys would say, "Just one more cast." All the boys knew exactly what that meant. Their departure would be delayed by at least several minutes. As far as the catch of the day was concerned, all fibbing aside, the stringer was not always filled to capacity. But who wants to carry a jampacked stringer all the way up Elm Street anyway? There were times, however, when the stringer was rather substantial. The boy remembers with great fondness fishing in the early morning hours before school. Had to be the spring of '62 or '63. The boy and his two buds, Mike and Bill, would proceed to the pier with a purpose. The bluegills, perch, and crappie were on the bite. The boy got to know Mike and Bill quite well and considered them best friends. They played sports together, pined over the same girls, and all three loved a good day of fishing on the Bay.

Mike and Bill could not be more different people. Mike was the bigger of the two, always sporting a haircut that was more like a close shave by today's standards. Mike liked sports and girls like everyone else, but he was made for the outdoors. He would have easily qualified as a "character." What the boy possessed in the way of shyness was trumped by Mike's extroversion.

Bill was about the same height as Mike but less substantial. Bill had an outgoing manner, charismatic perhaps. In a word, Bill was his "own man". Example – Surrounded by rabid Packer fans, Bill was a Detroit Lions fan. Bill loved the Chicago White Sox in spite of living an hour away from Milwaukee County Stadium, the home of the Milwaukee Braves. Thus, Bill's hero was Nellie Fox, who played 2nd base for the White Sox, the same position Bill adopted. The boy and Bill often found themselves competing for the attention of the same girl (Bill always won out) or being companions on the baseball teams all the way into high school.

Back to Spring fishing. On a number of occasions, the boys would complete a good harvest and briskly make their way up Elm Street. The purpose was two-fold: drop the fish off on the back porch for the boy's mom to clean and then make it to school before encountering the tardy bell. All was well and good until the boy's mom put a moratorium on dispensing with the fish in that fashion.

The old man continues to enjoy his 180° view and beyond. As he turns his head to the left, he has an unobstructed view of the beach. The boy remembers the beach house dominated the beach landscape back then. It was a simple gray structure with a flat roof. The lifeguards would perch themselves on the roof for a panoramic view of the beach. The clean brown sand could be seen up to the water's edge. The boys did not spend a lot of time at the beach, actually. The boy could swim, but not expertly. He loved water but not for the purpose of swimming. The same went for his chums.

Across the street was actually the main beach attraction. It was a small, old, weathered structure that faced the beach house on the opposite side of the road. It was known as the Snack Shack. The "menu" included hamburgers, hotdogs, shakes, and, of course, popcorn. The snacks were not the main fare, at least for the boy's best bud. His chum, Mike, had an obsession with pinball machines. On any given summer day, he could hear the "rat-a-tat-ding" passing through the old wooden screen door. The Snack Shack was the only place in town, or for miles, no less, that possessed those coin bandits. This simple little building had a charm all of its own. What wasn't so charming was the shaking of the building whenever the Chicago Northwestern train passed behind on its way to the nearby depot.

As the two look out over the Bay, the old man feels at peace – the boy, not so much. The boy remembers the Bay being primarily populated by serious fishermen in small or modest-sized boats. An occasional annoying water skier could be seen in the afternoon hours. Today, in his view, the scene is busier, almost frenetic. Probably what bothers the boy most is the fact that he is not armed with his usual array of fishing gear. He is certain that the big one that got away is still prowling the deep.

Although the two could spend hours staring out across the water, maybe it is time to journey back to the park. The two retraced their steps and crossed the old wooden bridge, then stopped to pay homage to the old willow tree that has stood the test of time. They find a bench near the water's edge and review the day. That uneasy feeling starts creeping in, followed by the question – Is this the last time the boy will ever return home again? While the old man dodges the question, the boy opens up his mental scrapbook once again. When the boy looks out at the Bay, he sees the various seasons come into play. The Fall season for two young outdoorsmen, the boy and his cohort Mike, was always eagerly anticipated. It couldn't come soon enough. The pheasants would be flying, and the rabbits would be seeking escape routes. It was one beautiful Fall day when Tom Sawyer and Huck Finn, on bicycles, thought their procession through town with shotguns draped over the handlebars would go unnoticed. That's what they thought, anyhow. As they rounded the corner on Walworth Street and headed down Geneva Street, they were abruptly detained by local law enforcement, specifically, Officer Ortiz, or as the boys often referred to, "Ocifer Oscar." Officer Ortiz informed the boys of his concern and issued not a citation but an edict: "When you boys ride through town and until you reach the village limits, gun cases are mandatory. Do you boys understand?" The boys got the message and felt relieved that no further action was taken. In the future, the boys would comply with the officer's directive.

Many of the boy's recollections relate to winter. Without much difficulty, he remembers ice skating, playing hockey, and ice fishing. He remembers walking down Elm Street with ice skates, sometimes a hockey stick over his shoulder. Once arriving at the Bay Shore, it was time to lace up the skates. Some years, it was so bitterly cold that it was impossible to wear enough socks or warm clothing to truly enjoy the day. The walk back up the hill didn't seem so bad after all. By the time the boy dropped his skates off on the back porch, he could feel the circulation in his extremities return. He remembers thinking maybe he should have gone sledding instead.

There was one winter, in particular, he recalls with special acuity. It started out with bitterly cold temperatures but not a wisp of wind. When the Bay froze, it was like walking on a windowpane. The ice was so smooth it was nearly impossible to walk on, but it made for exceptional ice skating. Aquatic vegetation was as visible as if being viewed in an aquarium. The winter remained quite cold that year in the early 1960's and the ice thickened considerably. Back in the day, the village would have a column of ice extracted from the Bay and place it on the corner in front of the barbershop. For all the village to see, it alerted everyone as to the conditions of the lake, specifically the thickness of the ice.

What would winter in the Bay be without the iceboats? Not knowing it at the time, the boy was immersed in what was probably the golden age of iceboats, races, and regattas. Lake Geneva was a legendary destination for those skippers interested in testing their skills. The boy was always fascinated with those sleek, speedy vessels. Powered by Mother Nature, they seemed to navigate the frozen terrain effortlessly.

The boy always wondered what a ride would be like but was too shy to approach one of the commanders. He does remember, however, one eventful day that made him reconsider his desire to ride in one of those projectiles on blades. It was a cold January morning. The boy was alerted that a gathering of fellow hockey enthusiasts would meet in front of the Bay Shore. After choosing sides, the match began. . It was a strange year. The Bay froze with sufficient ice to allow for recreation of all kinds of typical winter activities such as hockey, ice fishing, and ice boating. While the Bay was frozen, the main part of the lake was open water. That particular day, the wind was of sufficient force to encourage the ice boat skippers to ply their trade. Abruptly, the hockey match was interrupted. One of the boy's teammates pointed toward the open water and recognized how close to danger an ice boat had ventured – oops, too close. The skipper managed to turn his vessel over in the chilly January water. The proverbial pregnant pause occurred wherein the skipper was eventually seen crawling over the mast and sail, enabling him to reach solid ice. Quickly, the shocked captain made his way safely across the ice, making it to terra firma. The boy's interest in any passage of such was diminished considerably.

As the old man grows a little restless, the boy hangs on for a brief few moments. Not to leave out the summer, the boy recalls short walks to Conference Point to visit "Plymouth Rock." For no particular reason, perhaps just something to do on a quiet summer day, he and a chum or two would take the short walk. The rock was truly fascinating to the boys. It was huge - the biggest rock they had ever seen. Deposited by a glacier and polished by weather and foot traffic, it defined Conference Point.

The trip to the Conference Point was frequent, but the real trip, the challenging trip, was the annual walk around the lake. On an agreed-upon day, the boy and his chums would meet in the park and begin their expedition just around sun up. It was a tradition; nobody seems to know why, but heading to Lake Geneva would be the first leg of the 26-mile journey. Just seemed to be the preferred first stop. By the time the boys made it around the south side of the lake and reached Fontana, the obvious question was contemplated, sometimes uttered, "Why in the heck did we do this?" Once arriving back home, the aches and pains were forgotten. There was a small reward for completing the journey. If alerted, the Lake Geneva newspaper would publish the names of the foolish participants.

The boy recalls two of those "walks" just like that occurred yesterday. Those, the first and last, were memorable but for quite different reasons. The first walk included the usual cast of characters with the addition of their chum, Tom (Buzz). This was the inaugural voyage for all four. The boys met up at the park at the appointed time and proceeded forthwith. Of course, Lake Geneva was the first leg. The boys reached the city in good time. The Lake Path, as it was known, intersected with a place called the Riviera. To the boys, it seemed to be a sort of iconic landmark. The prominent red brick building had a long open-air hallway that allowed access to the lake. That corridor housed a gathering of pinball machines. It actually looked like a huge parking garage, but instead of cars, the stalls were occupied by more pinball machines than one could imagine. Mike, with his penchant for the devices, could have been crowned Pinball Wizard before the term was fashioned by the Who. The trip was in jeopardy as Mike saw no reason to journey onward. The remaining members of the expedition conferred, contemplating the only two realistic choices – forge ahead or turn back (with their tails between their legs). Push on, they did. Nightfall was approaching as they rounded

Conference Point. The trip was completed sans Mike, but he did make it home safely. A record of their journey could be gleaned from the Lake Geneva newspaper.

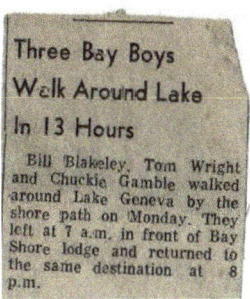

Three Bay Boys Walk Around Lake In 13 Hours

Bill Blakeley, Tom Wright and Chuckie Gamble walked around Lake Geneva by the shore path on Monday. They left at 7 a.m. in front of Bay Shore lodge and returned to the same destination at 8 p.m.

The second attempt to complete the 26-mile walk turned into a jog. The boy and his chum Bill made the trip in six hours. Having left the park at around 6 AM, the two boys eventually rounded Conference Point, this time to be greeted by the noon whistle. The boys were elated and could hardly believe their ears. It took some real convincing when the two discussed their feat with some of their chums.

The time now to exit the park and proceed up the hill to "downtown." The term downtown was used to describe just a handful of buildings and associated businesses. There was a unique geographic configuration to downtown Williams Bay. There was the Geneva Street portion that was hilly and housed the post office, dry goods store, and hardware store.

Around the corner and slightly down the hill were the businesses that occupied Walworth Street. This is where the boy and his chums spent most of their social hours. On one side of the street was the barbershop, grocery store, and "drugstore." It wasn't really a drugstore, but it was stocked with what one would expect to see in a drugstore sans the pharmacy. There were various items of interest, sundries they were called. More importantly for the younger patrons, it had a generous selection of candy bars that came in all sizes, shapes, and flavors. The majority of these treats could be purchased for a nickel, but some fetched a whole dime.

The drugstore, or Amundsen's as it was known, was the social epicenter of the Bay. The centerpiece of the store was, of course, the soda fountain. The offerings included just about every beverage a youngster desired. Coca-Cola would have been considered the "house drink," but malts, shakes, sodas, and phosphates were on tap. The boy often enjoyed wetting his whistle on a lime phosphate—"I would like a Green River please". For a mere ten cents, he was imbibing the nectar of the gods. Eventually, the boy's tastes became more sophisticated and spendy. When he began delivering the Beloit Daily News, his earnings could afford him a chocolate malt, a double chocolate malt no less. Served in the big metal canister, the boy would nurse the delicacy to the last lump of ice cream clinging to the bottom of the shiny vessel. The long, narrow soda counter was accompanied by several strategically placed stools. The stools were made of heavy metal and swiveled. Sometimes, to the annoyance of others, the stools could be spun at a high rate of speed.

Although the usual customers at the counter were under the age of eighteen, on occasion, an adult would seat him or herself so as to indulge in one of those tasty beverages. There was one adult, however, that qualified as a regular. Periodically, this younger gentleman of ample proportions would enter this juvenile stronghold and seat himself at the counter. He was quiet, not necessarily unfriendly, just quiet. The boy can never remember him engaging in any sort of conversation. The boy and his chums nicknamed him "Bubbles." It wasn't, believe it or not, meant to be rude. Rather, it simply represented a habit of his the boys picked up on. When the gentleman would seat himself at the counter, the boys often grimaced. They often wondered how the stool accommodated the rather large gentleman and did not give way. Without exception, "Bubbles" would order a "Bromo," short for Bromo Seltzer. The Bromo was dispensed by the attendant – two glasses, one with a dry powder and one with water. Bubbles proceeded to pour the water into the glass containing the medicinal powder. Back-and-forth, back-and-forth, until a frothy beverage was acquired. Bubbles proceeded to down the liquid and unceremoniously exited the establishment. The young boys are not exactly sure as to the purpose of the magic elixir but later learn it has something to do with calming the stomach.

Across the street from the drugstore were two very popular businesses. One was known as Stacy's, Stacy's Delicatessen. The boy remembers walking in the front door of this establishment and being greeted by a cooler stocked with a variety of frozen delights. Sometimes, it was downright hard to choose. Do I want a Popsicle, Fudgesicle, Push Up, Juice Bar, or Dixie Cup? If the boy was able to get past the cooler unscathed, he would encounter the main attraction. Next to the old manual cash register was what appeared to be an endless selection of penny candy. Once again, the boy was faced with a host of difficult decisions. Usually, through the process of elimination, he was able to satisfy his sweet tooth. The boy remembers times when he and his sister would sneak out of the house after washing the Sunday dinner dishes. Off to the delicatessen they went. Upon completing their mission, they were walking back up Elm Street with pockets full of those sugary gems.

Next door to the delicatessen was a very special place – Andersen's Bakery. It wasn't difficult to tell when the bakery was open, as the unmistakable aroma of fresh baked goods traveled from one street corner to the other. Unfortunately, back in the boy's day, the bakery was only open on weekends, sometimes only Sunday mornings. On special occasions, usually after Sunday mass, the boy would be summoned by his father and sent to the bakery to buy six Danish delights. These were very special Danish. They were baked in the shape of figure eight so as to accommodate two servings of jam or jelly. The boy could not wait to get home with his purchases. He hustled back up Elm Street as if he was chasing a fly ball in center field. Upon arriving home, the anxiously awaiting family members each secured one of the baked goods. Then things got a little tricky; there were six Danish but five family members. The problem was quickly dispensed with wherein the father, a.k.a. "big man" (his sister's term), made an executive decision.

A visit to downtown would not be complete without a walk up the Post Office steps to frequent the hardware store. Why the hardware store? Hardware stores are not normally an overwhelming attraction for young people. This boy, on the other hand, often visited the store even if he was without funds. All it took was him, and sometimes, his chums to pass through the front door and engage those squeaky wooden floorboards. Not far, just off to his right, represented the sole purpose of the visit. Under a small glass counter was the treasure trove of fishing tackle. The boy relished the thought of including a number of those items in his tackle box. His tacklebox was small and always understocked (underfunded). After all, no nimrod, young or old, would go to the Bay without at least a Daredevil, French Spinner, Black Nightcrawler, and Johnson Silver Spoon.

The boy mentally exited the store and moved towards the iconic Post Office. To a young boy, there is nothing particularly special about the Post Office - actually kind of boring, just a place to pick up the mail. It wasn't so much the Post Office; it was what was in front of the building that garnered the boy's attention and the attention of many others. The front of the Post Office constituted a ledge that hung over the steps leading to the lower part of town. It was a perfect location for an observation post so as to see traffic, motor and pedestrian, coming down Geneva Street while having an unobstructed view of the park. The boy and his chums might bring breakfast or snacks and shimmy out on the ledge, at least until they were evicted. The postmaster was quite aware of the popularity of this perch, so he was frequently required to expel the squatters.

In the late part of spring, the boy and his schoolmates observed a time-honored tradition. Following the school dismissal, usually around 3:30 PM, the boys would hurry down

Geneva Street and park themselves on the ledge if unoccupied. At the very least, they would seat themselves on the Post Office steps. Either one provided a good view of what was to come. From their vantage point, they could see the parade of students moving down Geneva Street, making their way towards downtown, many of whom were destined to frequent the drugstore. Amongst the gaggle of students was a special girl. She's pretty to a fault. But like the boy, very, very shy. The boy is now in his eighth-grade year. His girlfriend (she doesn't know it) is a seventh grader. As she got closer, she briefly glanced over at the boy, and the boy returned the favor. Quickly, the glances cease, and the uneasiness of eye contact shortens their imaginary visit. Over the number of iterations of these meetings, no words were ever exchanged, just the young beauty slowly passing by, clutching her books and three-ring binder as if they were going to be taken from her. The boy is hopelessly smitten. He wonders if she likes him or if it is just wishful thinking on his part. This ritual is observed until school lets out for the summer. He thinks about her often but never sees her during the summer months. He missed her shy, subtle smile, always neatly dressed, sporting those long, blonde pigtails. He does kick himself at times and regrets never having said a word to her. The fear of dismissal or outright rejection trumped any risk of verbal engagement. And so, the boy's first love, as is often the case, was brief and unrequited.

That memory is put to rest for now. The boy wonders, "Where next? ". In whatever direction he looks, there is a seemingly endless array of mental pictures or stories to retrieve. The mental slideshow is never organized or tidy. Why, at any given moment, one visual image takes priority over another will always be a mystery.

Why does the old man, for example, wake up in the middle of the night and see a past photo having nothing to do with the previous day's events? They just emerge for no rhyme or reason. The old man doesn't mind. The memories of his growing up in the Bay are always gratifying. Oddly, over the span of the boy's nearly five years in the Bay, he cannot recall a single negative event.

There is a part of town, not yet visited, that has its own special place in the boy's heart. A trip toward the Fieldhouse is obligatory. The boy logged countless trips down that narrow, tree-lined street. No matter the purpose of his travel, the boy was required to pass by the Arctic Circle. A town fixture, it was located in a shady area, which provided relief from the hot summer sun. There were no accommodations for indoor seating, but the outside wooden picnic tables sufficed. The boy did not know the owner personally, but he liked him. After every Little League game, each and every player was given a frosty mug of root beer. Better yet, if a player got an extra-base hit, he was rewarded with fries and/or a hamburger – for free! Past the Arctic Circle are two places of interest, one which the boy could claim having spent countless hours. The ball fields, both baseball and football, were located at the end of the road near the Fieldhouse. First - the baseball field. It was the only ballfield in town, so it had to accommodate youth to high school varsity baseball. The boy was obsessed with baseball. From his days of Little League, to his high school baseball days, he donned the respective uniforms and prowled that field.

When the boy was not playing ball or practicing, he was buying and trading baseball cards with fellow addicts. For a mere nickel, a pack of five baseball cards could be purchased. The contents even included a slim, brittle slab of bubble gum. All of his chums had much the same opinion: that bubblegum couldn't hold a candle to Double Bubble or Bazooka. Every pack of cards was opened with great anticipation. Always a mystery - Who did I get this time? Like his chums, he was hopeful of acquiring his favorite star. The boy's all-time favorite was Hank Aaron. The admiration was so intense the old man actually named his Black Labrador- "Hank" in honor of the great man. More often than not, there was a disappointment: "Darn – I already have that guy." Duplicates weren't all bad. They provided trading and bartering opportunities with his fellow junkies.

Back to baseball - in the boy's day, it was often referred to as hardball. The boy looked forward to gameday, much like he waited for Christmas to arrive. The boy's preparation for the big game (all games were big games) started hours before the actual game time. He was, on gameday, excited from the moment he woke up. The time leading up to the game would drag on and on. The boy would try to find something to do to kill time until he put on the uniform. One thing he could not do was go to the beach. Swimming, or not, by coach's edict "no swimming on game day or else" – translation "Don't let me see you guys near the beach."

Eventually, the boy would put on that scratchy wool uniform. From the socks on his feet to the cap on his head, everything was wool. With uniform on and glove in hand, the boy hopped on his bike. Down Elm Street to Walworth Street, he went. He always made a point of riding through downtown, hoping to be recognized by loyal fans. Maybe he would hear a cheer - "Go get 'em, Charlie" or "Have a good game, Chuckie!"

Eventually arriving well ahead of schedule, the boy would meet up with fellow teammates and prepare for battle. This ritual went on for a number of years, culminating with a varsity letter in his freshman year, presented by Coach Scherff.

Bordering the ball fields was the Fieldhouse. Periodically, the Lions Club would open the building so dances could be held for the youngsters. The boy attended a number of dances at this venue. The music was provided by the attendees, wherein anyone could bring their 45s. The dances, back then, possessed a cadre of unwritten rules. Not mandated officially, the boys usually occupied one side of the room, the girls the other. That arrangement made for some awkward moments when, by custom, the boy traversed the wide-open spaces (something akin to walking barefoot across a hot bed of coals) in hopes of getting a "yes" to the question "Do you wanna dance?" For some, like the boy, the journey across the room could be treacherous. After all, if his request for the honor of a dance was rebuffed, it would be a long and embarrassing trip back to his seat.

The boy especially remembers one fortuitous evening, or so it seemed. In that same Fieldhouse, the boy mustered up sufficient courage to pop the question. Across the great expanse, he walked and beseeched a tall (much taller than himself) blonde to dance. The boy did not know the beauty well but did see her brother at school. Better yet, the boy played baseball with the girl's brother. That, he thought, should count for something. The boy, that fateful night, was not sure what had gotten into him, but his courage was rewarded. She uttered the magic word- "Yes," and off they went to the dance floor. Not only did the boy dance once, but his confidence was increasing as the couple danced several dances in a row.

Ostensibly, all was well. So far, the evening was a success. Without warning, one of the boy's best pals asked the same young lady for a dance. Much to his chagrin, she accepted. The boy was now without a dance partner for the remainder of the evening. No dance partner; no potential girlfriend. Unbeknownst to the boy, history was beginning to be written. As fate would have it, his chum and his former dance partner eventually married. So much for the fond memories of the Fieldhouse. All in all, the boy harbors a cadre of fond memories about the various dances he attended. Dances were quite popular back then, a way of spending time during those long winter months. Although a card-carrying wallflower, the boy frequented the Fieldhouse, VFW, and a variety of private locations where dances were held.

As far as the pursuit of that elusive girlfriend was concerned, all was not lost. Since leaving grade school behind, the one thing sorely missed, by a bunch of hyperactive boys, was recess. But, the noon hour did provide a break from the books and allow time for pickup games – usually football or basketball. In the colder, more inclement days of spring, the gym was a noon gathering spot for junior and senior high students.

The boy and his chums enjoyed shooting hoops and showing off for the girls. After several days of "indoor noon recess," the boy's eyes drifted toward one particular young lady. She stood out from all the rest. His eyes trained on that beautiful dark shoulder-length hair – hair as dark and shiny as obsidian. That aside—she was pretty. Period. Even though the boy was drawn to this attractive stranger, his shyness and outright fear of talking to the opposite sex trumped his yearning to initiate a conversation. There had to be a way. With a little Yankee ingenuity or, in this case, Bulldog ingenuity, a solution was in the offing. Somehow, accidentally on purpose, an errant basketball headed her way. Upon intercepting the runaway orb, the boy approached, "Thank you… I'm Chuck…" The ice was broken, and the boy realized he had an unknown admirer all the time. This girl, Nancy, would become the boy's first girlfriend. The early awkwardness gradually melted into comfortable, typical teen conversations. Like any teen, lunch was always eagerly anticipated, but now with special purpose. As the boy was a freshman and Nancy was an eighth-grader, they had no common classes and, thus, could only see each other during the noon hour. For the time being, that would suffice. Over the days and weeks, the two conversed while forging a very simple, honest relationship – she liked him, and he liked her.

It was one of those chilly Spring Wisconsin days – the two met in the gym as usual. Much to his surprise, his sweetheart asked if the boy would meet her after school – sounded OK. "You mean your house?" It wasn't that he didn't want to accede to her wishes. Simply – he was petrified. "You mean meet your mom?" What could be more fear-provoking?

Nancy lived out on Cedar Point. The boy knew the area but not well. That was the other "neighborhood." His home turf was generally confined to the Conference Point side of the Bay.

The boy's apprehensions were put to rest quickly. Her mom was warm and welcoming. The visit went well, and the boy was readying himself to return home. Not quite – As he was about to leave, Nancy asked if he would accompany her to the lake path. Teeth chattering, he held her hand as they made their way through the tall leafless oaks. Abruptly, she came to a halt. Oh-oh. He never kissed a girl before. Well – what's the expression "He stole a kiss"? Didn't matter who stole what; his long walk home was dominated by thoughts of his friend.

The two young teens would continue their daily meetings until the end of the semester. Nancy was the quieter of the two

– a good listener, which the boy appreciated. Sometimes, they said very little – just sat and enjoyed one another's presence. It was good.

Footnote – After the boy's departure from the Bay (June of 1964), the two would never see one another again. The boy carried a torch for a while and would always wonder – "I wonder if she remembers me?"

After a rather full day of traversing the Bay and thinking of times gone by, the journey back is just on the horizon. The trip, as always, has been fulfilling. Those trips do come with somewhat of an emotional price, however. A plethora of fond memories is always salted with a measure of melancholy. Is it the passing of time? Is it the interruption of his adolescence? Is it the chums having never been revisited? Probably all of the above. The old man understands. The young boy has yet to face those life hurdles.

The requisite drive up Highway 67 is impending. It was in 1964, on a beautiful June day, when the boy's father made the announcement. The family was moving. This time, it was to the unknown of Green Bay, Wisconsin. At first, it did not quite jibe with the boy. Green Bay– why Green Bay? Had to be the greener pastures of a new job, he surmised. It still did not sink in with the boy, or he didn't want it to. After all, he just completed his first year of high school, kind of had a girlfriend, and earned his first varsity letter. For once, the boy felt like he was part of a tapestry. School was going well, and, more importantly, he had a wealth of friends. He felt he belonged somewhere and was accepted. Now – "We're moving?"

The boy remembers little about pulling away from the house, his home for the past few years, gratifying years. Still in a daze, stunned really, he could not yet accept he was leaving his chums behind. Gradually, slowly, the boy felt a sense of overwhelm. Not long after pulling away from the curb, Highway 67 came into view. It is a straight stretch of highway with a view all the way to the top, where Highway 67 meets Highway 50.

Up the hill climbed the small white Chevy station wagon. The kids and dog occupied the backseat of the vehicle. Without looking back, the boy was holding back tears, but to no avail. He protected his view from his parents and two siblings. The boy felt a terrible lump in his throat and a pit in his stomach. The crest of the hill was imminent. The required stop honoring traffic from Highway 50 was complete.

Camelot was in the rearview mirror.

Epilogue

And so that's the short version of the boy's growing up in what he has always considered home, his hometown of Williams Bay, Wisconsin. The author has no illusions as to the literary quality of his composition – a Pulitzer it is not. His trips back home have been many over the past fifty years. The last few have become more emotionally difficult, however. Going back to one's home is not just engaging the tangibles. It is not just identifying the old structures and remembering who lived where or what businesses were here or there. The emotional challenge is not what is here or there; rather, it relates to who is no longer with us. And so, when he goes back, he is faced with the stark, uncomfortable reality. Most of his closest buds are no longer with us. The author walks, views, sits, and reminisces with no one to pose the question, "Remember the time we…?" Nonetheless, he returns to the nest as needed, always worried it will be his last. Much like that trip up Highway 67 in June of 1964, he departs. At the top of the hill, as before, he finds himself looking in the rearview mirror.

He remembers them all. The names Mike, Bill, Ted, Doug, Dennis, Tom, and Gary are indelibly etched in this nostalgic mind. No two were alike. Each played a key role in his life. Each and all contributed to the boy's sense of belonging. The old man has saved just a few pieces of the memorabilia. Although the passing of decades has caused some attrition, a few pictures, class pictures, and faded Brownie photos of the Elm Street house remain.

There is, however, one very special item he has kept and treasured since his departure from the Bay. Remember Mike – the pinball wizard Mike? The boy's relationship with his brother-in-arms went much further than watching him rack up points at the expense of his favorite pinball machine. The two played organized sports together, but they were virtually joined at the hip when it came to the outdoors. The boy and his bud Mike fished the waters of the Bay year-round and hunted nearby fields, chasing rabbits and pheasants. Back to his prized possession. A day or two before the boy's departure from the Bay, Mike presented him with a brand spanking new shooting iron, a Springfield single-shot .22 rifle. That gun, still in his possession, has survived the trials and tribulations of the various moves and relocations over the years. From Wisconsin to Idaho and a number of destinations in between, that keepsake requires special reverence. Although a memento reminding the old man of good times has passed, it is not yet a mantelpiece. His grandkids have been instructed on the proper use of firearms and can be heard saying – "Grandpa, can we shoot the .22?" Assuredly, Mike would be proud. The old man can only assume Mike procured sufficient funds through "voluntary" contributions to purchase the going away present.

And so it is – a novice writer (using the term writer loosely) recounted growing up in a small town nestled in the glacial moraines of southern Wisconsin. It was written with an unwavering sense of respect and appreciation for his hometown and its people. There was, however, a hidden agenda that should be daylighted. It is sincerely hoped a reader or two will be prompted to reach out to an old chum. The rewards that go with reconnecting are immeasurable. Guaranteed – the gesture will be welcomed, and the discourse will invariably include "Do you remember the time…?"

Miss you guys.

P.S. The author, now in his 70's, is a thousand miles and fifty-plus years from home. He would give his eye teeth to borrow for a few days, even a few hours, HG Well's Time Machine. He would love to hop on that faded green bike of his and retrace his favorite route to downtown. He can see himself speeding down Elm St., turning left onto Walworth St. with the idea of meeting his pals at the "drugstore," aka Amundsen's. Not to be, of course.

The House On Elm St.

Brother Dan with Spike

A backyard birthday with Grandma Mcdonald Mrs. Peterson's home in the background

The boy, siblings Dan and Jodi, with black Lab - Spike

Bay Lions Little League

Bay Little Leaguers Gain Two Victories

The Bay Little leaguers took on the Sharon ball club last Tuesday and gained an 8-4 decision. Gary Gustavson did the hurling for the Bay, and pitched shutout ball after the first inning. Gary gave up six hits, eight walks and struck out seven. The Bay got eight hits and managed to get 10 free passes from Sharon pitching. Bill Blakeley received four, good for two runs.

Sharon jumped off to a 4-0 lead in the first on three hits and two walks. The Bay got one of those back in the second on a walk to Mike Crump, a stolen base, and a hit by Scott Burch. They scored two more in the third on a walk to Blakeley, and hits by John Kullberg, Crump, Burch and Dave Zabler.

The locals wrapped the game up in the fourth with five more runs. Chuck Gamble and Blakeley walked to put two men on. Back to back singles by Kullberg and Crump scored two runs, and they scored themselves as Sharon committed three consecutive errors.

Box Score

	ab	r	h
Gamble, cf	2	1	1
Breen, 1st	2	0	0
Blakeley, 2nd	0	2	0
Kullberg, c	4	2	2
Crump, ss	3	2	2
Burch, 3rd	4	1	2
Zabler, rf	2	0	1
Gustavson, p	2	0	0
Frey, lf	1	0	0
Johnson, lf	2	0	0
Martin, rf	0	0	0
Lawrence, 1st	2	0	0
Dahl, p	1	0	0
Menasco, rf	0	0	0

Circa 1961

Win Two In Row

The Bay Little leaguers made it two in a row last week when they beat Lyons-Springfield 6-2 on the home diamond. Jeff Stevens started on the mound for the Bay. Dennis Dahl relieved him and got credit for the victory.

The Bay managed seven hits and three walks off the visitors pitching. They got one run in the first on a lead-off single by Bill Blakeley and a long triple to left by Scott Burch. Chuck Gamble's walk and a double to right by Stevens put the Bay ahead 2-0 in the second. Springfield tied it with two of their runs in the top of the third.

Dahl's double in the Bay third was the big hit as the Bay went ahead to stay 4-2. They scored two more in the fourth on hits by John Kullberg and Mike Breen and a walk to Mike Crump.

Scott Burch played a good defensive game at third base for the Bay Lions.

Box Score

	ab	r	h
Blakeley, 2nd	3	1	1
Burch, 3rd	4	0	1
Crump, ss	1	0	0
Kullberg, c	2	1	1
Johnson, lf	3	0	0
Lawrence, 1st	1	1	0
Zabler, rf	3	0	1
Gamble, cf	2	1	0
Stevens, p	1	0	1
Gustavson, p	0	1	0
Breen, 1st	1	0	1
Frey, rf	0	0	0
Osborne, rf	0	0	0
Dahl, p	1	0	1

Row 1: T. Cooper, D. Dahl, E. Sundermann, C. Gamble, B. Johnson, E. Blakeley, S. Burch, R. Senior Row 2: M. Martin, B. Boe, D. Cramer, S. Stevens, A. Smith, D. Greenleaf, N. Lane, R. Blakeley, J. Giovanetti, Coach Scheff

Bulldog Baseball 1964

Palmyra Beats Bay

Williams Bay—Palmyra wrapped up second place in the Indian Trails baseball standings with a 9-4 victory over Williams Bay Thursday afternoon.

Gordie Holzhauer and Dennis Nicks combined on a four hitter for the Panthers.

Jeff Adolf had a double and single for Palmyra, while Nicks contributed a pair of singles and Tom Marsh a double.

Palmyra	AB	R	H	Williams Bay	AB	R	H
Nicks,p	4	1	3	Gamble,ss	3	0	0
Adolf,ss	4	1	2	Smith,cf	3	0	0
Anka,3b	3	2	1	Schlatt,p,ss	3	0	1
Marsh,1b	4	1	1	Stevens,1b	3	1	0
Henderson,rf	2	1	0	Blakely,lf	3	1	0
Geo,2b	3	1	0	Giovanetti,c	3	1	1
Gunther,cf	3	1	0	Blakely,2b	2	1	0
Heckhausen,c	2	1	1	Johnson,3b	2	0	0
Totals	31	9	8	Totals	22	4	2

Score by innings
Palmyra 000 333 3 — 9 8 0
Williams Bay 000 210 1 — 4 2 6
2B—Adolf, Gamble, Marsh. SO—Holzhauer 4, Schlatt 2; Nicks 4, Blakely 4.

1964

Bulldog Nine Edges Cadets 15-14 Friday

Williams Bay's youthful baseball squad edged the Northwestern Academy nine in a 15-14 slugfest Friday. The Bulldogs collected ten hits, and profited from a streak of wildness by the cadet pitching staff. Jim Giovannetti, sophomore pitcher-catcher, collected a triple and a double, and raised his team-leading batting average to .454.

The victory ran the Bay's Indian Trails record to 2 - 0.

WILLIAMS BAY (15)	ab	r	h
Gamble (ss)	3	1	0
Stevens (1b)	3	3	0
Blakeley R. (lf)	3	2	2
Giovannetti (p)	4	2	2
Blakeley, B (2b)	3	1	0

Eighth Grade

The eighth grade started out the year by winning the homecoming float competition.
The class worked cooperatively with the seventh grade in many social affairs. Between the study of American history and concentration on vocabulary building, modern math, and science, 8th graders are confident that they will be able to assume the responsibilities of high school in the years ahead.

Row 1: C. Gamble, B. Blakeley, T. Wright, G. Barner, G. Gundersen, M. Martin, S. Raberhorst, P. Nicholson, J. Nicholas, M. Lovell, L. Cox Row 2: Mr. Street, J. Soplenda, C. Frey, D. Dahl, P. Billing, J. Lamb, B. Kudrna, R. Anton, S. Burch, Mr. Guite Row 3: C. Rasmussen, D. Caldwell, J. Messer, J. Hukmann, I. Ingersoll, M. Rehak, O. Bach, P. Couzon, T. Casper, Row 3: C. Stenus, D. Henderson, G. Stevens, B. Williams, J. Delap, L. Cairns, A. Smith, J. Kullberg, J. Schultz, K. Seeley

Mr. Street's Eighth Grade Class

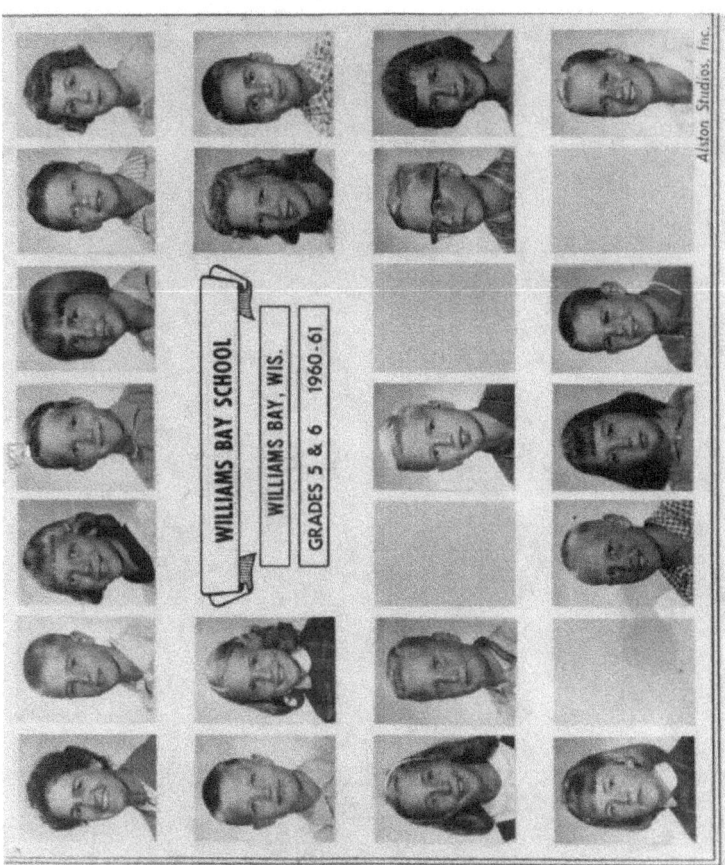

Mrs. Eliot's Class

Acknowledgments

The Author would like to thank all of those individuals who lent assistance in the completion of this project. Thank you Katherine—your word processing skills far and away surpass the author's high school typing abilities. There were many folks that read, reviewed, and critiqued the manuscript. Thank you, Ted, Allen, Robert, Bill, Rick, Michelle, Jodi, Nancy, Joe, Jane, and Pete. Last but not least, a big thanks to Deb. Her endless hours administering the two Williams Bay Facebook sites bring countless people back home, back to the Bay—Williams Bay, Wisconsin.

About The Author

The author was born in Beloit, Wisconsin. While in the fifth grade, the author's family moved to Williams Bay, Wisconsin, a small village on the shores of Lake Geneva. Although the author moved numerous times while growing up, he always considers Williams Bay his true home. The author now lives in Northern Idaho with his wife of 48 years and his two Labrador Retrievers - Hank and Libby.

www.ingramcontent.com/pod-product-compliance
Lightning Source LLC
Chambersburg PA
CBHW052206110526
44591CB00012B/2103